Heavier Than the Heavens

(The Everlasting Assets)

By

Bernard Benson Sarfo

Also by Bernard Benson Sarfo

The Fact Among Facts (1st)
The Fact Among Facts

Standalone
The Youth Murderer
Be Original Not a Copy
The Christians Science or Scholarship
Precious than Paradise
Habit makes future
A shelter from storm and rain
The Science of Life
The Strongest Lion Knockback
The Perfect and Inspiring City
Above Hope, Faith and Love
The Hero's Brave Decisions
The Weakest Among Plants
The Hero's Brave Decisions
Doing Above The Ability
The Wisdom Beyond Power And Greatness

Heavier Than the Heavens
The Academics Brains and Recreation Logics

Table of Contents

But we know that when he appears, we shall be like him, for we shall see him as he is. No one can explain this love of God towards us. | We need not to worry about anything concerning our lives. The whole Heaven has sacrifice for us to live again. What again that needs to be done for us to appreciate this love of God? Consider this text again; in Philippians 2:5-11

Dedication

I dedicate this book to everyone in the world today and wish them salvation!

Dedication

I dedicate this book to everyone in the world today and wish them salvation!

Considering this Scripture Always

'When wisdom entered into your heart, and knowledge is pleasant unto your soul, discretion shall preserve you, understanding shall keep you' (Proverbs 2:10, 11).

Introduction

Our hope as human beings lost about six thousand years ago. It's left us death; disease, hunger, poverty, hardship and so on. These resulted by our first parents sin. The penalty of this sin was second or everlasting death.

We lost hope as human beings. In fact, this kind of sin damages our being which resemble God's. There was no replacement which could be made for human to resemble God's again. Our situation was horrible to have the solution.

There is nothing that God can do to solve or replace His image that has come damaged. It's left to Him (God) to create someone again which resemble to Him and lose the first image and likeness as him forever.

Creating other image like Him was not His problem. But to lose that first image and likeness of Him became His burden and its trouble His heart. There was nothing that could solve this condition that Adam has brought it. He who knows the end from the beginning made provision to solve this problem in case it happens. He prepared himself and keeps watch, because of the will of a man.

It's wasn't His surprise because He already know and have prepared for that. Though, God could made different image and likeness like him, but He consider and maintain the first one through love and care.

That sin of Adam demanded blood which is innocent and not any other except the blood which is equal to God's to solve such penalty. Moreover, in order to solve this death penalty that Adam sin has created, God needs to become like a man and be subject to the rules that were first given to man.

If this is not done; the man cannot be restored to his image and likeness of God from the beginning. It took God to become a man and live as a man.

Jesus who is God accepted this condition and became a man born under the law in a set time. The sin of Adam made God a man to restore his position as a manager of creation again. It was a terrible decision made by Jesus. He is now a man forever and His condition cannot be exchange to God again. He became one of us and lived as any man.

God has change into a human being because of love. Who will accept and exchange his or her nature and live like a goat? Who will accept this condition for the sake of his or her animal?

Though, human beings were created in the image and likeness of God, but not as the same flesh. Our nature and structure resemble like God, but not in the same flesh and blood.

Jesus accepted to live as a man with the same flesh and blood. He was God and all things were created by Him. There was nothing that was made was out from His permission.

He made us hopeful again and accepted our condition as He who committed that sin and die for us. It's Jesus humans' hope and life giver. Let us consider this act of God and cherish it day and night. And then accept it deeply.

What shall I say to the people of the world today? Who can tell the end situation of this world? Why many people are struggling for the world goods that profit nothing? There are many people who say they know Christ but do not do what He says.

Many Christians in the world today are disk Christians but not real ones. Others deceive by taking His name for money sake. Many people are mention Christ name day and night but not in truth. Why are you deceiving yourself?

Do you know what is coming? What are you doing to yourself? The word is coming and that word cannot be mention by the scholars and it cannot be explain by the wise men. Why are you joking before a lion and why do you want to provoke the king of the forest?

Do you want peace or war with warrior? What are you doing? It's seems there is no judgment or the Creator of this world?

Many people want to live as they wish and then take Christ as their age mate who does not care anything. Many people also have heard Him but they do not regard Him at all. There are a lot of religious convictions in the world, are they all truly following Christ?

Many take Christ as the son of God; others take Him as a prophet who was sent by God. Some people also believe that He is an ordinary man like us who Mary gave birth to Him. Others too do not know who Christ Jesus is.

Those who say they know Him, even does not know who Christ Jesus is. Many other people use His name for jokes. Some also use His name for money sake. Who is Christ Jesus at all? Why must we follow Him and believe Him diligently?

He is the word of God; the word that God used to create the universe. There is nothing that was made surpass that word (CHRIST). The world was created through Him.

In the beginning there was a word and the word was with God and the word was God; all things were created through Him. He is everything that you need!

The world was created by Him. He is the author and finisher of everything. What are you searching for? Who do you need most or what man does the world need most? Why are you searching for things that profit nothing?

Is there anything that is necessary than Christ Jesus? What thing do you need that He lacks or cannot do for you? Who do you think He is or what have you thought of Him (Christ Jesus)?

What do you know and what do you want to know? What do men say about Him or what do you think of Him?

If you are in the world today, then know that it is through Him that you exist. Without Him you are nowhere and cannot be anything. What do you want to know about Christ Jesus and how have you consider Him?

Contents

1. It's Jesus

Who will accept to die for his or her dog which has stolen somebody's meat or exchange his or her life for an animal to live? There is no love that is greater than someone who will exchange his life for someone or his friend.

Who will accept to be poor for someone sake? Who will accept to sleep outside for his servant to sleep his or her room throughout his or her life? This is unconditional love that Christ Jesus accepts to die for mankind!

Oh! My dear have you consider such a love reveal by Jesus Christ for us? Why innocent will accept to die for a murderer? Who will accept to die for a thief who has stolen someone's property?

He (Jesus Christ) accepted to die eternally for the sake of a man. In the set time, God sent His son to redeem those who are under the law. He became a man and lived amongst us; though He is God but counted it as nothing. He was subject to die on the cross. He despised shame and die for the sinners. He put aside His glory and lived as ordinary man for the sake of mankind. He accounted His life as nothing and became as nothing for a man.

He became a lamb which takes away the sins of the world. He suffered for a man to have freedom. He died an eternal death for man to live everlasting life.

Who can do likewise and will accept this condition that Jesus Christ makes? Have you have heard of such incident as Jesus did before? Adam who committed his sin and deserve death could not understand the love that Jesus revealed.

Angels of Heaven were shock about this love and now they do not understand. Who is mighty that can stand before fire for the sake of his friend? Who will carry the burdens of a murderer who is on his way to crucify? Let us consider this scripture; Isaiah 53:1-10 read;

Who has believed our message and to whom has the arm of the Lord been revealed? [2]He grew up before him like a tender shoot, and like a root out of dry ground. He had no beauty or majesty to attract us to him, nothing in his appearance that we should desire him.

[3]He was despised and rejected by mankind, a man of suffering, and familiar with pain. Like one from whom people hide their faces he was despised, and we held him in low esteem.

[4]Surely he took up our pain and bore our suffering, yet we considered him punished by God, stricken by him, and afflicted.

[5]But he was pierced for our transgressions, he was crushed for our iniquities; the punishment that brought us peace was on him, and by his wounds we are healed. [6]We all, like sheep, have gone astray, each of us has turned to our own way; and the Lord has laid on him the iniquity of us all.

[7]He was oppressed and afflicted, yet he did not open his mouth; he was led like a lamb to the slaughter, and as a sheep before its shearers is silent, so he did not open his mouth. [8]By oppressionand judgment he was taken away. Yet who of his generation protested? For he was cut off from the land of the living; for the transgression of my people he was punished.

[9]He was assigned a grave with the wicked, and with the rich in his death, though he had done no violence, nor was any deceit

in his mouth. [10]Yet it was the Lord's will to crush him and cause him to suffer, and though the Lord makes his life an offering for sin, he will see his offspring and prolong his days, and the will of the Lord will prosper in his hand.

Just consider this situation that Jesus been through for our sake. He did nothing that deserves punishment. But he wished to die for us to live. Will you consider and do something about it? Or this is nothing before you, oh my dear never be a lost person, because Christ Jesus has done it all for us.

He was punished for our peace and die for us to be restoring again. It's Jesus; that is why it's Jesus! He was crucified for us and dies the second death for us. What will you do for Him and what is your love? It's Jesus; consider and trust Him and be a thankful everyday concerning His love towards us!

2. The Lamb of God

He is the acceptable Lamb of God and the sin bearer for our sake. He was subjected to death from the beginning of this creation. He was the lamb that was slain the first time Adam committed sin in Eden.

He is the beloved son of God and the only begotten son. He who believes in Him should not perish but have an everlasting life. He was born by Virgin Mary whom Joseph married. He is the son of man and the son of God.

The sin of Adam created sacrifices for the remission of sin each day and night. The situation was burdensome for the Israelite's to even afford for those lambs that needs to be kill for sin pardon.

Christ Jesus made it once for our sake and the sake of the world that whoever believes in Him will have his or her sins pardon. He is the lamb without blame and perfect for the sacrifice. He made it once and forever.

He open the way that leads to God and made it possible for us to be accepted. For by grace we have been saved through faith, not by works but by faith that no one should boast. He is the light of the world and the world could not accept Him. He came into His own but they did not understand Him. Through Him we receive grace and have grace.

The world was created by Him and He is God. He is the Lamb of God which takes away the sins of the world.

In fact, Jesus Christ has done everything that needs to be done for human salvation. Our duty is to accept Him as our savior and Lord; and then to live according to His instructions.

We do not have any work to do to be accepted by Him. It is by grace but not by works that anyone should boast. Our part is to allow Him to lead; then we follow. Anyone who believes in Him will not perish but have an everlasting life. If we will continuous sit in Him.

He is meek and low in heart; and he wants us to follow Him in the same way, and then takes His yoke and burdens. He has done it all; there is nothing that is left for us to do to make it perfect. It is already perfect and acceptable to God.

Follow Him as He makes His steps. You need not to follow Him with your other opinion or what you think is good to be added. You just follow with your step that is all your duty. You cannot do anything, but by Him.

He is the Lamb of God and the acceptable Lamb. You are not the lamb for the sacrifice. So, what do you want to do concerning the sacrifice that you do not understand? God wish this sacrifice than the Abel sacrifice. It is total and there is no need to have another. He has done it all.

Christ is our only hope; the grace and the truth. His sacrifice is not as any gift or goods devoted for God to be use by His servants, but it is His blood that brings forgiveness of sins of the world and the life of those who will believe in him.

Who has believed our message and who has revealed the arm of the Lord for us to see, for He came out as a tender shoot? He was less recognized and has no beauty to be cherished, but He carried our sins to the cross and His soul has saved many.

He is our substitute and the carrier of our burdens. He was like sheep in the hands of slaughter. Why? It is because of our sins He accepted to carried and bear the punishment. Oh! My dear, have you thought of such loved that Jesus Christ shown to us?

He is our replacement who carried the doom life for us and accepted to die eternally for us to live perpetually.

He is a good shepherd and laid His life for the sheep. In fact, His love cannot be explain and understand it. He buried our souls on the bottom of His love and covered with His compassions.

He is a wonderful savior and advocator willingly to help at all circumstance of our life. He died and now alive forever more. He has done the greatest of love which surpasses every love that we know and can share to our love ones.

He is the Lamb of God that takes away the sins of the world. For God so love the world and gave His only begotten son, that whosoever believe in Him should not perish but have an everlasting life.

Christ Jesus is the lamb that takes away your sins. Will you accept His sacrifice and love shown to you? What will you do for Him? He is the Lamb of God for replacement of your doom life. Will you consider?

3. The world destiny key

Our hope as human beings lost and we became hopeless through the sin of Adam. We became useless and void. That is, a dust that cannot be used for anything again. Adam lost future hope and joy of his life.

This situation wounded God and pears like arrow in His heart. The whole intention of God missed the right position and it became useless as intended. But God who knows the end from beginning made the plan equal to the first and honored it again.

Here our hope as human beings missed its target and joy. Our situation as human beings subjected eternal death; diseases and poverty and so on. Our fate as human beings exchanged negatively, and it became horrifying day and night.

Doors of hope closed eternally and the joy of a man stood aside. The condition of a man became abysmal and he was eternally ceased to live. Oh! Is there hope for a man again? Can a man survive again? What way can a man pass to have his nature that has lost for eternity? Can we be hopeful again? Which way can a man pass and gain his lost perfect nature?

Who can exchange this condition for a man and how can we receive it? Jesus Christ made a way for escape and solved it for man! He is our peace and has broken the walls of afflictions that closed the access for our peace and joy.

A door of joy that was closed by the sin of Adam has been open by Jesus Christ. He has made the access to God so easy and comfortable.

He holds the keys of death and hades. He is the world destiny key and without Him; no world, no life and hope or expectation for anything.

He is the key; the door, the way, the truth and the life. Our success depends on Him; our joy depends on Him, our peace depends on Him and the others.

He is fountain of the living waters and the bread of life. He is the means that justifies the end. He is all in all. He is the indispensable key that opens doors for successes. Who wants to live a life that is meaningful?

Who has determined to live a worthy life? Who wants to upgrade his or her life? He is the key for all these doors and without Him, there will be no profit. Our ways and life depends on Him for success.

The hopeless situation of a man became meaningful by Jesus Christ. The lost expectation was restored by Him. He became our hope and redeemer of all our conditions.

He was tested in all points like us and He is able to help those who run to Him. He is the great object of life that everyone must seek for. He restored the broken images and the likeness of God which Adam lost for eternity.

He is our way and everything. The world cannot survive without Him. It is His wish that we live and have our being. He is our comforter and joy of hope. Let us consider Him and be at peace. For He is the one who our fate has been established. Do not fear but have faith in Him!

4. Who is worthy to open the scroll?

Our hope has been certain in Christ. The cry and the worry of John the revelator have been answered.

John the revelator cried in his dream when he couldn't found the one who is worthy to open the seven seals of God for the destiny of mankind certainly established.

The whole world is in trouble; the time is coming where no one can survive comfortably. Our destiny has a question that needs the answer. Sin has changed the direction of our life. We are all in trouble and yet the questions to be solve.

Who can stand and answer these question that concerning life and death? Oh world! There is a case on it way coming.

The world needs to be destroying and rebuilt again by God. But there must be a remnant that needs to be establishing again to God for eternity.

This cannot be done, unless the seal of God that holds this world destiny open by someone; not just anyone but the one who is worthy.

The worthy one should not be an Angel of Heaven who knew no sin. But a man likes Adam who is blameless and has lived in the world with flesh and blood but without fault or anything that is called sin.

That person is the only one worthy to open the seal of God for the world to have its proper cloth again. The penalty of sin cannot be solved by Angels of Heaven. It needs a man to solve it for a man.

Jesus Christ accepted this condition and became a man to solve man's problem. He became a man with all sorts of trials that leads a man into sin. But He stand firm with no sin and committed all His case and everything to God.

He was accuse and persecuted by men. He faced all circumstance that leads to sin, but He did not sin. He was accuse with false pretends and the end nailed Him on the cross.

With all sorts of accusation, He closed His mouth as a sheep in the hands of a slaughter. He did this for the sake of a man. Who can explain this kind of act that Jesus revealed in His life?

He made it for the sake of mankind. He was rejected by a man for the sake of a man. He was pears by a man for the sake of a man. He nailed to the cross by a man for the sake of a man.

He did all for a man to be restoring again. It came to pass, John the revelator cried in his dream for he did not find the one who is worthy to open the scroll of the seals of God for the sake of a man.

Every good and precious thing did not talk but those that are good for nothing talks a lot. Jesus waited and delayed a bit to see what will John the revelator will do.

He shake his faith to see if John the revelator still believe that He (Christ Jesus is and is able to open the scroll of the seals for man assure of his salvation.

One of the elders in John's dream told him to cease cry, because the lion of Judah the seed of David is worthy to open the scroll of the seals for man salvation reassured.

Christ Jesus is worthy to open the scroll of the seals of God. He died and alive and holds the keys of death and hades. He has bought us with His blood and He is alive forever more to advocate for us.

Jesus is our only hope for salvation. There is no other thing or a person needed to be saved through him. Our good works cannot save us; our love shown to others cannot save us.

There is nothing but Christ Jesus can save us. It is He only but not the other. He is worthy to open the scroll and lose the seven seals of God. Let's read the Bible and think of the seals and the one who is worthy to open and lose it. Read;

Revelation 5:1-14

Then I saw in the right hand of him who sat on the throne a scroll with writing on both sides and sealed with seven seals.

[2]And I saw a mighty angel proclaiming in a loud voice, "Who is worthy to break the seals and open the scroll?"

[3]But no one in heaven or on earth or under the earth could open the scroll or even look inside it. [4]I wept and wept because

no one was found who was worthy to open the scroll or look inside.

⁵Then one of the elders said to me, "Do not weep! See, the Lion of the tribe of Judah, the Root of David, has triumphed. He is able to open the scroll and its seven seals."

⁶Then I saw a Lamb, looking as if it had been slain, standing at the center of the throne, encircled by the four living creatures and the elders. The Lamb had seven horns and seven eyes, which are the seven spiritsof God sent out into all the earth.

⁷He went and took the scroll from the right hand of him who sat on the throne. ⁸And when he had taken it, the four living creatures and the twenty-four elders fell down before the Lamb. Each one had a harp and they were holding golden bowls full of incense, which are the prayers of God's people.

⁹And they sang a new song, saying: "You are worthy to take the scroll and to open its seals, because you were slain, and with your blood you purchased for God persons from every tribe and language and people and nation. ¹⁰You have made them to be a kingdom and priests to serve our God, and they will reignon the earth."

¹¹Then I looked and heard the voice of many angels, numbering thousands upon thousands, and ten thousand times ten thousand. They encircled the throne and the living creatures and the elders.

¹²In a loud voice they were saying: "Worthy is the Lamb, who was slain to receive power and wealth and wisdom and strength and honor and glory and praise!"

[13]Then I heard every creature in heaven and on earth and under the earth and on the sea, and all that is in them, saying:

"To him who sits on the throne and to the Lamb

be praise and honor and glory and power,

for ever and ever!"

[14]The four living creatures said, "Amen," and the elders fell down and worshiped.

Jesus has done it all and our hope has been curtained. My dear! Let's consider this act of Christ Jesus and do something about it. He is worthy and accepted by God for us to be considering again. What is the seal and what is it about? Read some of it: Revelation 7:1-3

After this I saw four angels standing at the four corners of the earth, holding back the four winds of the earth to prevent any wind from blowing on the land or on the sea or on any tree.

[2]Then I saw another angel coming up from the east, having the seal of the living God. He called out in a loud voice to the four angels who had been given power to harm the land and the sea: [3]"Do not harm the land or the sea or the trees until we put a seal on the foreheads of the servants of our God."

Let us notice some event in it in Revelation 8:1-13.

Read;

When the Lamb opened the seventh seal, there was silence in heaven for about half an hour. [2]Then I saw the seven angels who stand before God, and seven trumpets were given to them.

[3]And another angel came and stood at the altar with a golden censer, and he was given much incense to offer with the prayers of all the saints on the golden altar before the throne,

[4]and the smoke of the incense, with the prayers of the saints, rose before God from the hand of the angel.

[5]Then the angel took the censer and filled it with fire from the altar and threw it on the earth, and there were peals of thunder, rumblings,flashes of lightning, and an earthquake.

[6]Now the seven angels who had the seven trumpets prepared to blow them.

[7]The first angel blew his trumpet, and there followed hail and fire, mixed with blood, and these were thrown upon the earth. And a third of the earth was burned up, and a third of the trees were burned up, and all green grass was burned up.

[8]The second angel blew his trumpet, and something like a great mountain, burning with fire, was thrown into the sea, and a third of the sea became blood. [9]A third of the living creatures in the sea died, and a third of the ships were destroyed.

[10]The third angel blew his trumpet, and a great star fell from heaven, blazing like a torch, and it fell on a third of the rivers and on the springs of water. [11]The name of the star is Wormwood. A third of the waters became wormwood, and many people died from the water, because it had been made bitter.

[12]The fourth angel blew his trumpet, and a third of the sun was struck, and a third of the moon, and a third of the stars, so that a third of their light might be darkened, and a third of the day might be kept from shining, and likewise a third of the night.

[13]Then I looked, and I heard an eagle crying with a loud voice as it flew directly overhead, "Woe, woe, woe to those who

dwell on the earth, at the blasts of the other trumpets that the three angels are about to blow!"

We need not to fear or shake for what is about to happening in our world. But we need to do something, and what is that thing?

If you are not truly the follower of Jesus, then decide now and accept and follow Him. That is what you need to do. He is worthy to open the book and break its seals for your sake. Will you consider? It's Jesus!

5. Our only hope

Oh! Why many people are struggling for peace in the world? Why many others have put their hope in the governments in the world today? Can a hopeless give hope or can a dead giant for a dead dog?

They all are the same and there is nothing that a dead soldier can do to a lives baby. Who is your hope? Why that person is your hope? Can he or she give to their fellow ones? Why are you cursing your life? Why are you harming yourself?

How can dead lion talk to a lives dog? A dead king and dead servant; who is bigger than whom? Two lines that ends in the same point, which is stronger and which is weaker? Two dead kings, who will bury the other?

Why all these questions that I am asking? There is no one on this earth who needs to be trusted or put our hope in him or her. We all like a flower which burns in the heat of a sun. We are like a vapor that vanishes in a minute. Who is important than the other? Who will last? Who can predict the end of the other? Who is our hope and must be trusted? It's Jesus Christ! He is our only hope and life giver. The world became darkness through the sin of Adam.

The glory of God which is our cloth vanished and we became naked. Our hope vanished and became hopeless. We were subjected to death and diseases. We lost the beauty and real nature of our being.

Our way of life became questionable and dismantled. Who will we cry to him or call for help? We were in the middle between nature and God. Who shall we run to for help? We have transgressed against God and nature cannot advocate for us.

We lost hope and became as nothing. Who shall we run to for help and pardon our transgression? It left to us but no redeemer to be look at. Our state as human beings became horrible and undefined.

Who will vindicate for us? Who will encourage us to be on our foot? The one who created us is merciful and abundant in goodness. Through His grace and mercy, He made a way of escape and restores us again. For we have no one to run to and have our peace. The world became darkness and has nowhere to turn to that will give us light for us to live again. Let us read something from Mathew 4:16, read;

The people who sat in darkness have seen a great light. And for those who lived in the land where death casts its shadow, a light has shined."

Our situation became darkness and empty. We stood on our foot not knowing where to turn. God called us again and have mercy on us. He restores us by His grace and compassion. Consider this Bible text: Isaiah 1:18 read;

Come now, and let us reason together, said the Lord: though your sins be as scarlet, they shall be as white as snow; though they be red like crimson, they shall be as wool."

Jesus makes us hope again by taken our flesh and blood. Live like us and subjected to the rules and regulations of a man and God.

This is great and awesome. He has broken the walls of affliction and has made it peace. He is our only expectation and savior. Who is your hope? Make Jesus your hope and everything and will not move or shake.

He has risen from the death and holds the keys of death and hell. He wants your life dear and wants to do everything for you. Listening to His words to you; Isaiah 55:1 read;

Ho! Everyone in need, come to the waters, and he who has no strength, let him get food: come, get bread without money; wine and milk without price.

He wants to set us free and make us kings; holy people and the priest of God. Who will you compare and be as same? Who do you believe? Who is your hope? Let's seek Him as he is near and we will find Him. Let's forsake our evil ways and come to Him.

Those who are labor and are weigh down with heavy laden, He will give you rest.

Read this quote Romans 8:38, 39 For I am persuaded, that neither death, nor life, nor angels, nor principalities, nor powers, nor things present, nor things to come, nor height, nor depth, nor any other creature, shall be able to separate us from the love of God, which is in Christ Jesus our Lord. He is our only hope and life giver.

6. The fountain of living waters

The source of life and exists of every nature depend on the spring of waters. The world came out from waters and nature needs water to survive. In the beginning God created the Heavens and the Earth.

The earth was formless and empty. The whole face of the earth was covered with waters and deep. Darkness existed all over the earth and there was no dry land to be planted. The light was absent to see ahead.

But water has covered all the space of the ground. God commanded the light to appear and its came as He commanded. Why waters in everywhere in the face of the ground?

The firmament as we see are waters and the earth has been combined with waters. Water is life for the nature.

That is all nature depends on water to survive. There is a life in the water and the growth. The living things on this earth grow and survive by water. Without water nature and earth cannot survive. There will be no growth without water for the creatures. God put life in waters for nature to use and survive. We human beings cannot survive without water and light.

God did these two elements for our progress and comfortable life. The trees; grasses of the field, seeds and vegetables depend water for growth and life. Naturally, the world and things in it live by water.

The man became a living being when God breaths on his nostrils. We became a living being the breath of God. The living things as we see survive or live by water as we live by the breath of God.

Everyone must notice this message that I am giving out or sharing by God grace. We depend on something to have our being or live. Without that, we cannot survive or live as human beings.

Our life depends on someone to have our being. Who is it or who is our source of life? Many people think that they can survive each day and night with their own strength and it is max or automatic to live by your strength. It is not so as they think. But there is someone who holds out our and make us lives every day and night. Who is that person?

It is Jesus Christ the son of God and only begotten who is in the bosom of the Father always make us live and have our being.

Never think that you own yourself and can do all things by your strength. Men, it is not so and cannot be anything without Him (Christ Jesus).

He is the life; the truth and the way. He is the fountain of the living waters that makes us alive day and night. Without Him, we will be nothing and cannot move or survive.

He is our source of life; the strength and the light. Without Him, there will no light; life and the living soul. We were nowhere and as nothing. We were dust which cannot be used for anything.

The world and the things on it were created by Him and it depends on Him to survive and have its beings. As the living things like a tree cannot survive or grow without water; so, we human beings cannot survive or live without Jesus Christ our Lord and Savior. He is the fountain of the living waters.

Means, He is the all source of life and the life giver. In Him was life and the life was the light of men. He is the bread of life and the water of life. What can I say again? Let us note something from the Bible. Read;

Revelation 22:1

He showed me a river of water of life, clear as crystal, proceeding out of the throne of God and of the Lamb,

John 4:14 Read;

But whoever drinks the water I give them will never thirst. Indeed, the water I give them will become in them a spring of water welling up to eternal life.

There are a lot more that I can let you know but time will not permit me for more. He is the source of everything that we will be needed. He is the life; He is the light, He is the water of life, He is the bread of life, He is the prince of peace and the everlasting Father. It is Jesus; Immanuel.

Our life depends on Him and without Him there will be no life. Whoever believe in Him and drink will survive eternally. Notice these Bibles texts and think about it. Read;

John 5:23 "Whoever does not honor the Son does not honor the Father who sent him."

John 5:42–43 "I know that you do not have the love of God within you. I have come in my Father's name, and you do not receive me."

John 6:45 "Everyone who has heard and learned from the Father comes to me."

John 8:19 "You know neither me nor my Father. If you knew me, you would know my Father also."

John 8:42 "If God were your Father, you would love me"

Will you consider and drink from the source of life? It is Jesus; your life, your way and the fountain of the living waters!

7. Immanuel

God became human being and live amongst human beings. His name shall be called Immanuel; means God with us or God is with us. Who am I talking about? Who is that person lived among men but God Himself?

God ways are wonderful and difficult to understand His doings. Why did God live amongst us? What transpired? We committed sin at the beginning of our existence against God. It took God's life to solve this problem.

It became needed for God to turn into a man in order to restore His image and likeness that man has lost because of sin. The world turned into darkness because of the sin of Adam.

The case of Adam was so dangerous and perplexed. The whole idea of God to a man changed and rotted through the sin of Adam.

The joy of Heaven ceased at the moment and sons of God mourn about this incident. What will Heaven do about this episode? The whole human race is at risk and the nature cannot live in peace for such situation. If there is a war, who must fight and lead? If the royal cease to fight, then servants will run.

The case became God case to fight for a man by His strength. This was not the hands and the cutlasses fight. But it is the war on sin. The war could not be a successful without the nature of a man.

Else, the war of sin cannot be a war for God. So, it took God to turn into a human being with flesh and blood as of Adam. Here, God became second Adam and lived with flesh and blood. Who will wish to become a fish in the sea water and then live as a fish throughout his or her life last?

This is what Christ Jesus did for man sake. He became a man and lived amongst men with the same blood and flesh. Though, He is God but counted as no reputation to be equal with God.

He humbled Himself as a servant and became a man. His love is great and incomprehensive. He accepted to live as a man and fight the battle of sin.

This is awesome decision and fabulous act. He won the battle on sin and has been honored with all power and the name above every name both Heaven and the earth and under the earth.

If God is for us, who can be against us? You should not worry and fear of wants. Why are you so fearful?

He (Jesus) has done it all and there is no other to be done again. He has finished the race for us and has fought and won the crown.

Read Romans 8:28-40

Read;

28And we know that in all things God works for the good of those who love him, whohave been called according to his purpose.

29For those God foreknew he also predestined to be conformed to the image of his Son, that he might be the firstborn among many brothers and sisters.

30And those he predestined, he also called; those he called, he also justified; those he justified, he also glorified.

31What, then, shall we say in response to these things? If God is for us, who can be against us? 32He who did not spare his own Son, but gave him up for us all—how will he not also, along with him, graciously give us all things?

[33]Who will bring any charge against those whom God has chosen? It is God who justifies. [34]Who then is the one who condemns? No one. Christ Jesus who died—more than that, who was raised to life—is at the right hand of God and is also interceding for us.

[35]Who shall separate us from the love of Christ? Shall trouble or hardship or persecution or famine or nakedness or danger or sword? [36]As it is written:

"For your sake we face death all day long;
we are considered as sheep to be slaughtered."

[37]No, in all these things we are more than conquerors through him who loved us. [38]For I am convinced that neither death nor life, neither angels nor demons, neither the present nor the future, nor any powers,

[39]neither height nor depth, nor anything else in all creation, will be able to separate us from the love of God that is in Christ Jesus our Lord.

Is there anything that deceiving your heart? What are your longing for? What is your problem? What is difficult that Jesus Christ cannot be able to solve? What is the matter? He has accepted and died ready for your sake.

What again do you need for Him to do for you and accept Him as your savior and Lord? He is Immanuel; means God with us. He became a man and died for a man.

He is alive and advocate for us. Do not worry about your sins that you have committed, but confess to Him, He will have mercy on you and forgive all your sins. For He is alive forevermore and pleading for you.

He is merciful and gracious and abundant in goodness. What's your problem? He is Immanuel! He is with you and will not forsake you or leave you. Will you mind?

8. The bread of life

As human beings food sustain our life; that is, we eat in order to survive. Food is life element for human beings. God gave us food to eat and to survive. Our body and spirit have their food and it is needed to make life dear and comfort.

Everyone must eat and to survive. Means it is necessary and cannot be avoided. Food is needed to make us cheerful. Bread is life for human beings and animals.

In fact, human beings work for food. That is, the main object of human's life is based on food. We all work for food to sustain our life. In all, we die at the end.

Why those foods cannot sustain our life for long. Why we have been created to eat and survive but die with the food we eat? Our nature today cannot be sustained by food eternally.

Some even die early because of diet. In all, what will help our life to sustain long and even eternally? Christ Jesus is the bread of life and the only hope to sustain human life for long and eternity. What is your food or diet? Which food do you always eat? What benefit have you got from it? He is the bread of life and His flesh is abundant of food.

He is the bread of life that came from Heaven. Everyone who eats of this bread will have life and it abundant. For His flesh are food and the life. You will ask in what way it can be?

The word of God is the flesh of Christ Jesus. Everyone who read and do as it has been said to him or her receive life and peace for his or her soul. We always eat but what is the benefit so far? Everyone who eats His flesh will have life and have it abundantly.

Have you consider the word of God? What have you read? Search the scriptures for in it you shall receive life and the rest for your soul. Why are you searching for food that profits nothing?

What have you got since you searched those foods? You need to work on the food that will sustain your life and it abundant. Our fathers eat manna which is the food of Angels of Heaven but they died. But Christ is the food that leads to life everlasting. You need have this food every day in your life.

Do not seek for food which cannot sustain your life everlasting but food that can sustain your life throughout eternity. That is the word of God which is Jesus Christ.

He is the bread of life and not just a life but life everlasting. Why don't you seek for Jesus instead food and why don't work for diet that will sustain your life for eternity?

I am not talking to you just we live our daily life every day. But I am telling you about the truth concerning the peak of life and it abundant or the real meaning of life and what it concern.

We do not know what we must know and do not do what we must do. This life that we are in is not life, but it is a vanity of life. Everything that we do is vanity and mind disturbing.

What profit can we gain from all the toil work that we are doing? It is vanity. We will not take to anywhere. We will leave it and go without profit. We will not carry anything into our grave. Yet we will be as nothing and useless.

Why are you seeking for dust instead of gold? Why are you seeking for weeds instead of seed? As human beings what do we need first in our lives?

What is before us and what will happen at the end of this world? We always worry about food and clothes that we will wear. We always seek for money and other things.

But what is the benefit of these things that we always seek for? Everyone is busy and do not have time for the precious pear that give life and abundant peace for the soul.

Our souls need something beyond compare and lasting. That is, Jesus the bread of life and the source of life. He is the word of God that give life and hope for hopeless.

Oh! Is there someone who can give hope and everlasting life? Yes; it's Jesus! He is your only hope and food that will sustain your life throughout eternity. You must seek for food that will give you an everlasting life. Consider these texts from the Bible. Read john 6:35

Then Jesus declared, "I am the bread of life. Whoever comes to me will never go hungry, and whoever believes in me will never be thirsty.

We need to seek for bread that is life and the water that will prevent us from thirsty again throughout eternity. That is, Jesus!

Let's read again John 6:25 -59

[25]When they found him on the other side of the lake, they asked him, "Rabbi, when did you get here?"

[26]Jesus answered, "Very truly I tell you, you are looking for me, not because you saw the signs I performed but because you ate the loaves and had your fill.

[27]Do not work for food that spoils, but for food that endures to eternal life, which the Son of Man will give you. For on him God the Father has placed his seal of approval."

[28]Then they asked him, "What must we do to do the works God requires?"

[29]Jesus answered, "The work of God is this: to believe in the one he has sent."

[30]So they asked him, "What sign then will you give that we may see it and believe you? What will you do? [31]Our ancestors ate the manna in the wilderness; as it is written: 'He gave them bread from heaven to eat.'"

[32]Jesus said to them, "Very truly I tell you, it is not Moses who has given you the bread from heaven, but it is my Father who gives you the true bread from heaven.

[33]For the bread of God is the bread that comes down from heaven and gives life to the world."

[34]"Sir," they said, "always give us this bread."

[35]Then Jesus declared, "I am the bread of life. Whoever comes to me will never go hungry, and whoever believes in me will never be thirsty. [36]But as I told you, you have seen me and still you do not believe.

[37]All those the Father gives me will come to me, and whoever comes to me I will never drive away. [38]For I have come down from heaven not to do my will but to do the will of him who sent me.

[39]And this is the will of him who sent me, that I shall lose none of all those he has given me, but raise them up at the last day.

[40]For my Father's will is that everyone who looks to the Son and believes in him shall have eternal life, and I will raise them up at the last day."

[41]At this the Jews there began to grumble about him because he said, "I am the bread that came down from heaven." [42]They said, "Is this not Jesus, the son of Joseph, whose father and mother we know? How can he now say, 'I came down from heaven'?"

[43]"Stop grumbling among yourselves," Jesus answered. [44]"No one can come to me unless the Father who sent me draws them, and I will raise them up at the last day.

[45]It is written in the Prophets: 'They will all be taught by God.' Everyone who has heard the Father and learned from him comes to me. [46]No one has seen the Father except the one who is from God; only he has seen the Father.

[47]Very truly I tell you, the one who believes has eternal life. [48]I am the bread of life. [49]Your ancestors ate the manna in the wilderness, yet they died. [50]But here is the bread that comes down from heaven, which anyone may eat and not die.

[51]I am the living bread that came down from heaven. Whoever eats this bread will live forever. This bread is my flesh, which I will give for the life of the world."

[52]Then the Jews began to argue sharply among themselves, "How can this man give us his flesh to eat?"

[53]Jesus said to them, "Very truly I tell you, unless you eat the flesh of the Son of Man and drink his blood, you have no life in

you. [54]Whoever eats my flesh and drinks my blood has eternal life, and I will raise them up at the last day.

[55]For my flesh is real food and my blood is real drink. [56]Whoever eats my flesh and drinks my blood remains in me, and I in them. [57]Just as the living Father sent me and I live because of the Father, so the one who feeds on me will live because of me.

[58]This is the bread that came down from heaven. Your ancestors ate manna and died, but whoever feeds on this bread will live forever." [59]He said this while teaching in the synagogue in Capernaum.

I know you have heard something from Christ Jesus mouth. You have read for yourself now. What are you doing about it?

What's your mind? What are you seeking for? Will you seek for Christ who is bread for your life or seeking for bread that cannot sustain your life for eternity?

He is the show bread that sustains the priest of old life. He is the light of the world that gives life for those who seek Him. He is the word of God that life to those who read. Without Him no one can survive.

You need this bread as the Pharisees said. He is the bread of life and everyone who eats this bread will have an everlasting life. It's Jesus but no other. Will you consider?

9. Who Jesus Christ is?

So, who is Jesus Christ at all? Why Jesus Christ needs to be known by everyone and trust Him? What is He at all? Does he have any records that are trustworthy or needs to observe again?

Is there any records or witnesses concern His life that makes Him different from the other religious founders? Is there anyone who has been able to rise from death as He? Who has been able to witness about himself as the real son of God apart from Him?

Who Jesus Christ is at all? He is the word of God that created the Heavens and the Earth at the beginning of this universe. He is the word of God and He is God. He is the way; the truth and the life. He is the savior of the world.

He is the Christ the anointed by God. He wasn't created but the Creator of the world and the second of the God's head. He became a flesh and was born by Virgin Mary. He is the Lamb of God that takes away the sins of the world. He is the resurrection and the life. He is the lion of Judah and the fountain of the living waters. He is the light of the world and the bread of life. He is the author and finisher of our faith. He is the Alpha and Omega.

He is the supporter and the lawyer for our destiny. He is redeemer and the hope for human race. He is Immanuel and the everlasting Father. Is there anyone who has been able to testify of himself about all these titles or claim as He?

Is there anyone who has been challenging or claim these titles before or after as He? Who has claimed it before or after him since the world came into existence? Who called these heavens and the earth or who has been able to say I was before Abraham and I was before the world was created?

No one has ever said these things apart from Him. He is the Messiah and the one who holds the keys of death and hades. He is the rock and desire of ages. He is the living one and was dead and now alive forevermore. He is Melchizedek who has no any mother or father or any genealogy. Who have these records concerning his life apart from Jesus Christ? He is the dear son of

God and the only begotten son who ever believes in Him would not perish but will have an everlasting life.

In the beginning there was a word and the word was with God and the word was God. All things were created by Him and there was nothing that was made without Him.

My dear, do you want any witness again in order to believe or have faith in Him? Who has ever claimed these titles before? Who can say these things about himself? Have you ever heard someone claiming these titles before?

He is and there is no one again! Many people are wondering and some of them are doubting concerning these messages about Jesus Christ. Some believe that He was a prophet of God. Others also believe that, He was a Mary son but live ideal life in the world.

He is the true vine and without Him you can do nothing. He does not need any Heaven Angel to testify about Him physically for us to believe Him! We does not need any evident to be trusted Him. He is the one who hang and died on the cross of Calvary.

Why all these comments my dear? There is no hope in anyone again, who can solve your problems and give you hopeful life and the everlasting life apart from Jesus Christ! He is the only way; the truth and the life. What do you need in life?

He is all in all and there is no expectation again. Through Him the world was created and without Him there was nothing made.

What do you need again? He is calling you to come to Him and have rest for your soul. Are you labored and have heavy laden, he will give you rest.

Seek Him first and things will be added unto you. He is the shadow and light for the Israelites in the desert some time ago. He is the rock that waters them when they became thirsty in the wilderness. Trust Him and put yourself in Him. He is your savior and the world redeemer.

He will never leave you or forsake you. Just relax and put your confidence in Him and be at peace. He became poor to make you rich and die for your sake.

Who do you need again and what are you searching for? He is the one that even sea listens to Him. The world and its goods cannot save you or satisfy you. You need to decide your life and the destiny you wish about this message that you are now reading through.

Who is your hope and redeemer? Jesus Christ and the world renowned founders are standing before you; who will you chose?

May God give you understanding about this matter and to make a better decision for your life! What again do you need apart from Him? Note these Bible texts;

I am the living bread that came down from heaven. If anyone eats of this bread, he will live forever. And this bread, which I will give for the life of the world, is My flesh

The next day John saw Jesus coming toward him and said, "Look, the Lamb of God, who takes away the sin of the world!

John3:36[1]

Whoever believes in the Son has eternal life. Whoever rejects the Son will not see life. Instead, the wrath of God remains on him

---

1. https://biblehub.com/john/3-36.htm

10. The world creator

In the beginning God created the heavens and the earth. The earth was formless and void. The Spirit of God move upon the face of the waters and the Lord said let there be light, and there was a light.

The world was nothing at the beginning; it was formless and void. That there was anything on it, except waters in the face of deep. The Lord prepared the world by His word; and that word which prepares the earth and makes it meaningful was Jesus Christ.

Note, Jesus was the word of God and the world was made by Him (The word). In the beginning there was a word and the word was with God and the word was God. Through Him the world was made and there was nothing that was made without the word.

So, Christ Jesus was the Creator of the universe. All things were made by Him and it was made for Him. There was nothing that came without Him. Who can tell how this world came about and who can proof of how it was all began? Christ Jesus is the one who can tell how it was started.

Through the world, He is the only one who has said something about creation and has confessed that the world and everything in them was for Him and it was created by Him.

So, He was the creator of the universe. Who can challenge Him concerning creation? Who has ever testified about himself as did Jesus said about creation that all things are His? Let's consider these Bible quotes: in John 16:12-15; what did He said: let's read:

I have yet many things to say unto you, but ye cannot bear them now. Howbeit when he, the Spirit of truth, is come, he will guide you into all truth: for he shall not speak of himself; but whatsoever he shall hear, *that* shall he speak: and he will show you things to come.

He shall glorify me: for he shall receive of mine, and shall show *it* unto you. **All things that the Father hath are mine: therefore said I, that he shall take of mine, and shall show *it* unto you.**

Jesus is the only one in the world history who has able to said these words. Let's read of them John17:10 Says; All I have is yours, and all you have is mine. And glory has come to me through them. Who has ever said this before throughout world history?

What witness do you need again to accept Jesus Christ as a Creator and the world redeemer? He is the Creator of the universe! He knows where He comes from and where He is going. Where the other founders do comes from and where are they going?

Birds of the air will tell you and fishes in the sea will let you know that Jesus Christ is the only one who can give you hope and everlasting life. He is the Creator and the life giver. All things belong to Him and were made by Him.

Let no one deceive you and never put your trust in any other founders who does not know where he or she comes from and do not know who he or she is going. What must I say to you again? Who knows the end and the beginning of this creation? Who has ever said of himself or herself that he or she and the Father (God) are one? Who has ever said this before? Except Jesus Christ; who is the only one in the bosom of the Father.

Many people have taken Jesus Christ as a messenger of God or a prophet who came and work as a preacher. In fact, one thing we need to know is that, who will be the ruler of this world at the end of this age?

What will be the reward of each one on this world? What must we do today to avoid eternal doom? The Creator of this world is coming to reward those who are in this world. You cannot escape the end reward right for your deeds.

He is the Creator of the universe and the life giver. He knows the ends from the beginning and knows the beginning to the end. He is the way; the truth and the life. There is no savoir apart from Him. He is the owner of this world and all things were created by Him.

He is the Christ the anointed of God. He is the only way to Heaven, the passport and visa of identity of Heaven representatives. He wasn't created by anyone but He is the one heads of the Creators. This means that, the Father, the Son and the Spirit are one in everything which they do. O hear Israel; the Lord our God, the Lord is one.

Deuteronomy 6:4 [1]

This world has the owner and He is coming to reward those who are on this earth. What is your decision concerning this matter? How do you understand the trinity of God as one?

Who has ever confessed that he is one with the Father? Consider this text from John 10:30 said by Jesus Christ. I and my Father are one. He is the one with God (The Father).

So, Jesus Christ is the Creator and the life giver, you cannot avoid Him and have life. He is the only one that you need to be accepted by God. He is the law giver and the light of the world. Never ever reject or put Him aside or regardless of Him.

Your life is in His hand and He can destroy and make you alive. Without Him you cannot have life and cannot survive. He is the Creator of the heavens and the earth. What are you doing about this message? Trust Him and have faith in Him. He is your only hope and the answer to all your problems.

11. The sin bearer

Oh! What a wonderful love and character which no pen can describe or explain by any human philosophy. God created the heavens and earth at the beginning and made all things ready for human being who was His likeness and image.

He was instructed to eat from tree and to guide the Garden of Eden. But he was forbidden not to eat from the tree of knowledge of evil and good. Adam disobeyed the instruction given by God.

There was a penalty concerning eating from the tree of knowledge of good and evil. A man was to face second death and

1. https://biblehub.com/deuteronomy/6-4.htm

punishment mainly for eternally. The hope and the joy lost for man and his entire descendant.

It was a tragedy matter which no one can solve except God Himself. How could this happened and it must come as such? The blood needs to pay this penalty and punishment. The angels cannot solve such a problem and condition of this incident. So, it turns to God to solve this case.

The purpose of God changed because of the will of a man. It was a tragic incident and no one can solve it. Oh! What a disappointment. The whole idea of God changed and it grieved him.

Is there anything that can make a change to make God satisfy? This is a dreadful situation that changed the entire world and its atmosphere. Who can solve this problem which is an eternal doom by his life? Who can explain this case and how can it be solved?

The entire Heaven goods cannot solve or paid for this penalty that sin of Adam has caused. Who can solve this problem that even Heaven goods cannot pay for? The only treasure that can solve this situation is the blood of God Himself.

This is the love of God it took His life to make a man whole again as he was at the beginning! This is terrible and uncalled for. What a condition and a big mistake that Adam did?

My dear, the situation was so abysmal and it is a mess to discuss about. Our way of life has changed and we always need God to make us at peace. Who will be our lawyer before God and who will die eternally for us?

Jesus Christ the only son of God and God Himself accept this situation and solve it by His blood which only can pay the price that sin of Adam has caused.

He was substitute for us and bears the sin penalty. He accepts it as He has done such a sin and would suffer for it.

There is no greatest love than this that someone will die for his friends. He bears our sins to the cross and paid the price by His blood which is the only treasure that can pay the price. Jesus Christ accepted to die eternally for us to survive.

This is very dear indeed and tremendous love no one has done it before from Heaven and the Earth. We cannot understand and cannot be interpreted by us or Angels.

Even Angels of Heaven do not understand this love of Jesus Christ and they cannot explain or find the bottom of it. He accepted to die eternally and does not value His kingdom dearly than us. He wanted to die eternally and to let us live eternally.

All we like sheep have gone astray; we have turned everyone to his own way; and the Lord hath laid on him the iniquity of us all.—Isaiah 53:6

Who can explain such a love and know the source and the foundation of it? How can a man die for mice? How can even a mad man be replace to die for a dog? How will you consider such a condition?

How will you want to die for a dog which has stolen somebody's meat? Can you be considered this matter? Oh! My dear, God died for the dust which is contrary to His form or body. He decided to die without profit and valueless His nature which is out from creation.

How can this be possible but Jesus Christ made it possible. He bears our sins and pays the penalty price. Many people do not understand the death of Christ and others do not value it.

Some also want more explanations in order to believe. My dear, if you look at you condition, what will you say about yourself as human being?

It is His grace that makes you alive today. You deserve death and punishment of your sins. But Christ Jesus has made it possible for you to receive the forgiveness of sin; will you accept His death and make Him your Lord and savior?

Note; let's read from Ephesians 2:8-9 "For by grace you have been saved through faith, and that not of yourselves; it is the gift of God, not of works, lest anyone should boast. We have been favored and honored by God through the death of Jesus Christ.

He (Jesus Christ) has made it possible for us to be accepted by God. Who are we that God love us so much? He accepted to be punished for our sin as He who has committed that sin.

Read this text 1 John 3:1 How great is the love the Father has lavished on us, that we should be called children of God! Dear friends, now we are children of God, and what we will be has not yet been made known.

But we know that when he appears, we shall be like him, for we shall see him as he is. No one can explain this love of God towards us.

We need not to worry about anything concerning our lives. The whole Heaven has sacrifice for us to live again. What again that needs to be done for us to appreciate this love of God? Consider this text again; in Philippians 2:5-11

[5]Let this mind be in you, which was also in Christ Jesus:

[6]Who, being in the form of God, thought it not robbery to be equal with God:

[7]But made himself of no reputation, and took upon him the form of a servant, and was made in the likeness of men:

[8]And being found in fashion as a man, he humbled himself, and became obedient unto death, even the death of the cross.

[9]Wherefore God also hath highly exalted him, and given him a name which is above every name:

[10]That at the name of Jesus every knee should bow, of things in heaven, and things in earth, and things under the earth;

[11]And that every tongue should confess that Jesus Christ is Lord, to the glory of God the Father.

Here Christ Jesus exchanges His body that is Holy and that was not created by anyone for the sinful flesh and dust that cannot be used for anything because of love and self-denial. He became a man and took upon him the form of a servant.

How do you appreciate such a character? How do you value and cherish it? Have you ever thought of this love before? What do you think of it?

We need no other evident that Jesus has die for us. It is bigger Heaven environment and dear than anything that can be diligently seek for. What again? Our eternal doom has been solved by Christ and we have chance to make it more profitable.

Read from Isaiah53:10

Yet it was the LORD's will to crush him and cause him to suffer, and though the LORD makes his life an offering for sin, he will see his offspring and prolong his days, and the will of the LORD will prosper in his hand.

What sin have you committed that God cannot forgive you? His grace is great and precious that any sin that has been committed by a man. He has devoted His life for us and he is there always to plead for us. He is faithful and merciful to forgive our sins if we truly disclose.

My dear, I can say a lot that cannot be counted and I can testify what you cannot imagine. But the true is to accept His dear death and make Him your Lord and savior!

You need nothing but Christ Jesus who disregards His deity and he you honor by His death. He is ready to solve all your problems just tell Him and ask for His guidance.

12. The resurrection and the life

Who has rising from the death before? Is there any history concerning someone who have rising from the death before? Can we have someone in the world history; who is that one and what is his name?

Since Adam committed sin at the beginning of his life in the world history, which caused the death penalty to mankind; have we heard of someone who has die and been buried for three days and has risen from death before accept Jesus Christ?

Someone will say we have some records for that, but it is not true. Those people haven't been buried, but they went to coma and survive again. Jesus Christ is the one who tasted the death and has risen from the death.

There is no doubt about it, and this proves His divinity and Lord of Lords. He raised Lazarus from death and other peoples. He holds the key of the death and hades. He can put His life down and take again. He is the bread of life and the resurrection and the life.

Who can challenge these messages and proves his records and facts that it is not so in the world history?

There are a lot of religious leaders who has come and died and gone. Those founders even do not know their stand in the day of reckon. Others came and deceive people for their own interest.

Some are even the agents of the devil but pretend to be the angels of light. Those leaders do not have any records concerning death and their life which surpass even the children die on their birth day.

Never make yourself a king and deceive people who are not learned. You shall reckon about it and receive your reward. Why this comments? In fact, there is no one who can save your life and can make you better.

Who have you put your hope into and who do you believe? Christ Jesus is the only one who can save your life and give you hope. He is the resurrection and the life. We have no one to put our trust in him; accept Jesus Christ who is the life giver and savior of the world. Consider this text and put your trust in Him.

Let's read; Jesus said to her, "I am the resurrection and the life. Whoever believes in me, though he die, yet he shall live, and everyone who lives and believes in me shall never die. Do you believe this?" *–John 11:25–26*

Who do you believe? Is it **Mohammed of Mecca who have died and gone?** Is it **Krishna** who appears to be part man and part supernatural entity capable of all sorts of remarkable things? He is no more to be found and do not even know his stand at the end of world.

Is it **Gautama Buddha** who doesn't know his stand today? I have many to say but time will not permit me to write more of others who are founders and well renown in the history of the world. Consider these founders who have been able to rise from the death?

Never trust any man or put your confident in him. These people are no more and they cannot be finding or look into them for help.

My dear, the only one who is alive today and can be trusted is Christ Jesus who is in Heaven today plead for our behalf to God to have mercy on us. Let's hear His voice and see who He is?

Revelation 1:18, "I am the Living One; I was dead, and now look, I am alive for ever and ever! And I hold the keys of death and Hades"

He is the first and the last; He is the living one, He was dead but now alive forever and ever. Who do you consider?

Who have helps you more than Christ Jesus? He holds everything including the keys of the death and the grave.

What's your mind concerning this message? Do you believe or you are thinking of it? He is the bread of life and word of that created the heavens and the earth.

Never take Jesus Christ as a mere prophet which other people think of. But take Him serious than anything that needs to be considered!

He is the way; the truth and the life, without Him no one can please or accepted by God! Consider this message and think of it. He is the resurrection and the life. Will you mind?

13. The way, truth and life

Do you have heard someone confessing that he is the way; the truth and the life before apart from Jesus Christ?

Who has confessed this statement before? What do you think of it? This book title is deeply concern this content. Its take Christ to please God: What do I mean or what do I want you to know?

In fact, a way is what leads us to our destinations. There can be no way without home or place of comfort.

If there is a way then there is a home. There are ways that leads to our cities and towns. Those ways that leads to our cities and towns are one when get to the entrance.

Why Christ Jesus is saying He is the way; the truth and the life. He means that, there is no one apart from Him who can make life dear and cherish. He also means that, without Him no one can survive. And He is saying; He owns everything which is in Heavens and the earth. He means there is no way again. This is serious message that needs consideration by anyone on earth.

He continuous says; He is the truth. What did He mean? He means that, those who have come cannot be trusted or relied on them. He means that, they do not have anything to give and then owns nothing.

They are not the way that leads to life. They are hopeless to be trusted. He further says; I am the life. He has finished the speech.

Who can challenge Him about these sayings? Who have said it before? My brothers and sisters; what miracle do you need to accept Christ Jesus as your personal savior?

He has finished the speech and there is no one who can continue. Our life depends on Him; our need depends on Him. He is everything that life needs and there is nothing that will be necessary apart from Him!

He is the way to Heaven; He is the way to life and He is the truth. He is above all and nothing can be compare. He owns life and owns riches.

He is the foundation of all knowledge and wisdom is His cloth. He is the rock without damage or spoil. He is the lamb which God accepted be to scarifies for our sins that needs pardon.

He is the true vine and the desire of ages. He surpasses all and He is God. What can you compare to Him? What is your prove? From east to the west; south and north, there is no way again that leads to eternal life.

Never search for weeds but search for gold that earn you something. Means do not follow those who do not know where they come from and do not know where they are going. I am done and I do not have any more to tell you.

Jesus Christ is the way; the truth and the life. Its take Him to please God. No human being can give you a life or can save your life. It is a big mistake to set your mind on human being who does not know his or her end.

Many people have failed and have wasted time for nothing. Where do you want your life and where do you want to go?

We need to have God's character in order to be accepted in Heaven. Jesus Christ is the one who can give you that.

He loves you so much and wants your life than His life. He is preparing a home in Heaven for you and you are dear to Him. Let's read His messages to us. John 14:1-14

Let not your heart be troubled: ye believe in God, believe also in me.

²In my Father's house are many mansions: if it were not so, I would have told you. I go to prepare a place for you.

³And if I go and prepare a place for you, I will come again, and receive you unto myself; that where I am, there ye may be also.

⁴And whither I go ye know, and the way ye know.

⁵Thomas said unto him, Lord, we know not whither thou goes; and how can we know the way?

⁶Jesus said unto him, I am the way, the truth, and the life: no man cometh unto the Father, but by me.

⁷If ye had known me, ye should have known my Father also: and from henceforth ye know him, and have seen him.

⁸Philip said unto him, Lord, show us the Father, and it sufficeth us.⁹Jesus said unto him, Have I been so long time with you, and yet hast thou not known me, Philip? he that hath seen me hath seen the Father; and how sayest thou then, Show us the Father?

¹⁰Believest thou not that I am in the Father, and the Father in me? the words that I speak unto you I speak not of myself: but the Father that dwelleth in me, he doeth the works.

¹¹Believe me that I am in the Father, and the Father in me: or else believe me for the very works' sake.

¹²Verily, verily, I say unto you, He that believeth on me, the works that I do shall he do also; and greater works than these shall he do; because I go unto my Father.

[13]And whatsoever ye shall ask in my name, that will I do, that the Father may be glorified in the Son. [14]If ye shall ask any thing in my name, I will do it.

This is His message to us and He want us good but not of evil. He is giving us hope and future. He is our only hope and life. He holds keys of death and hades. He is the dear son to God. All power has been given to Him.

He is our lawyer; He is our advocate; He is our life and salvation. He is our sin bearer and redeemer. The Heaven and the can teach you more about Christ and His duty to mankind. Consider this text and think of it. Let's read;

Revelation 3:20-22

Listen! I am standing and knocking at your door. If you hear my voice and open the door, I will come in and we will eat together.

21Everyone who wins the victory will sit with me on my throne, just as I won the victory and sat with my Father on his throne.

22If you have ears, listen to what the Spirit says to the churches.

I hope you have learn a lot and I wish you will do something about immediate as possible. May almighty God bless you and be considerate about this message.

14. All in all

It is very wonderful and difficult to understand God. It is not easy to describe the nature of God and understand His presence on earth. His works are wonderful and very deep to discover. He is everywhere on the globe at the same time.

Can you imagine how things grow without seeing it with your naked eye? This is the Lord we serve; He above comparing or describing His being because no one has ever seen Him personally before. He is above everything but He is Humble.

Christ Jesus became flesh and lived among us. He took upon Himself human nature and became servant. He disregards His nature as God and wish to be a servant for the sake man's life and dignity. Who can describe the love of Christ Jesus?

Who can tell reasons why He decides to die the unreturned or second death for a man? In fact, the highest and beauty of love and anything concerns love is to be selfless. It is the character surpasses character and everything called kind. It holds everything and there is nothing that can be comparing with. This is the nature and the attitude of Christ Jesus.

That is why all power has been given to Him by God and His name has been raise above all names both Heaven and earth. Who will die for thief or who will die for a murderer who deserves to die by his or her sin?

Jesus Christ accepted to die without remembrance for Adam and his children after him. The beauty of this attitude move God to raise His name above every name from Heaven to earth and under the earth. Who can be comparing with Him and who has ever done such before?

It is beyond good and what is called upright. Angels of do not understand the selfless nature Jesus Christ and they love to do what they can to support such a wonderful character to recue human race as did Christ Jesus wish.

That is why Christians are guided by Angels of Heaven. Christ Jesus is everything and He is above needs and wants of a man. He sacrifices His life for no profit and died a second death without of hope of resurrection.

He is dear son of God and only begotten son that whosoever believe in Him should not perish but have an everlasting life. Let's read

John 1:4, 5

In him was life, and that life was the light of all mankind. The light shines in the darkness, and the darkness has not overcome it.

He is the life and the light of all mankind. What must I say to you that you will believe Jesus Christ that I am writing about Him?

You can ask from end to the end of the world that there is no one who saves apart from Jesus Christ. Consider this text Acts 4:12 let's read:

Salvation is found in no one else, for there is no other name under heaven given to mankind by which we must be saved

Salvation is in no one else under the heaven given to mankind that we must be saved. Here Jesus Christ is the only who can save us from our sins and is He who God has accepted for us to be save through Him.

He is all in all and everything we need. He has done everything necessary for our salvation. He is our hope and has opened a way for us to be accepted and have our needs.

Read from Hebrews 4:16 Let us then approach God's throne of grace with confidence, so that we may receive mercy and find grace to help us in our time of need

We need not to worry about the matters of life but what must we be worry that our salvation is certain in Him?

Oh! What can I say again? The religious leaders cannot be our hope of salvation. They have no life in them and cannot be our hope. Do not trust anyone but Christ Jesus who is the resurrection and the life. It is my hope that you will understand this message and do something about it. You need nothing but Christ Jesus who holds keys of death and the hades. He is your only hope of salvation and everything that you need. He is all in all.

15. Is there anyone again?

Is there anyone who can save people from their sins? Who is that person? What is his name? Is it Mohammed of Mecca? Is it Krishna? Or is there anyone who is equal to Jesus Christ? What do I want you to note and keep in mind?

There is no other person who can save you or can be trusted. We have no savior apart from Jesus Christ.

He is the door; the keys and the house for refuge to all mankind. He is our richest; the fame and the glory. He is the beginner and the finisher of our faith.

He is the Architect of the world and the things that are in. He holds every power and authority. All things were created by Him and will be destroy by Him. It is His will that we exist and have our being. He can put His life down and take it again.

Who can challenge Him and be like Him. He is the Alpha and Omega and the fountain of the living waters. He is the good shepherd and the owner of the sheep. What is your idea and what do you think of it? Whom shall we follow? Who can we trusted?

It is Jesus Christ who die on the cross of Calvary and rise from the death. He holds the keys of death and the hell. He is the life; the truth and the way.

What do people say and how do they take Jesus Christ for? Some say He is a prophet; other says He is one of the prophets.

Another group says He is the son of God. Others also say He cannot be a son of God, because God does not have a wife to born for Him.

My dear, whether you will accept Him or not and say whatever want to say about Him. I want you to know that, without Him (Jesus Christ) you have no life. Then and again you can do nothing and can be nothing without Him.

Do not let any religion deceive you or take some teachings that is contrary about what the Bible is saying about Jesus are not a mere thing.

The evidence is Christ Jesus is the way; the truth and the life. I tell you, this is all. He is the one that you need and He is the only hope for mankind. Let's read some scriptures from the Bible: 1John 5:1-10

Read;

1 Everyone who believes that Jesus is the Christ is born of God, and everyone who loves the father loves his child as well.

2 This is how we know that we love the children of God: by loving God and carrying out his commands.

3 In fact, this is love for God: to keep his commands. And his commands are not burdensome,

4 for everyone born of God overcomes the world. This is the victory that has overcome the world, even our faith.

5 Who is it that overcomes the world? Only the one who believes that Jesus is the Son of God.

6 This is the one who came by water and blood—Jesus Christ. He did not come by water only, but by water and blood. And it is the Spirit who testifies, because the Spirit is the truth.

7 For there are three that testify:

8 the Spirit, the water and the blood; and the three are in agreement.

9 We accept human testimony, but God's testimony is greater because it is the testimony of God, which he has given about his Son.

10 Whoever believes in the Son of God accepts this testimony. Whoever does not believe God has made him out to be a liar, because they have not believed the testimony God has given about his Son.

Who do you want to believe? Why do you want to believe that person? What does that person has done to you? Is He the created of the universe? What is his position? Did he have life and exist today? What is his age? Who is that person? What is his name? Where has he comes from?

Oh my men do not let someone fool or deceive you. If it is not Jesus Christ, stay in your poverty. But if it is Jesus Christ, then rejoice and put powder in your hairs and jump from end to end and say it is Christ; it is Christ Jesus!

Let the world hear you by saying; it is Jesus Christ! Do not let anyone disturb you about Him. Do not fear to proclaim His name.

He is the one you really need. No one again; no one again and there is none who can give you a life. It is only Christ Jesus who can make you whole and necessary. Consider this scripture and be at peace.

Isaiah 9: 6-8

read; **6** For unto us a child is born, unto us a son is given: and the government shall be upon his shoulder: and his name shall be called Wonderful, Counselor, The mighty God, The everlasting Father, The Prince of Peace.

7 Of the increase of his government and peace there shall be no end, upon the throne of David, and upon his kingdom, to order it, and to establish it with judgment and with justice from henceforth even forever. The zeal of the LORD of hosts will perform this.

8 The Lord sent a word into Jacob, and it hath lighted upon Israel.

You need not anyone but Jesus Christ! No one again; no one again but Jesus is the only one you need. That is all!

16. The Everlasting City

Why everlasting city? Will it collapse? Will there be any city again? What this city stands for? Who will be the leader; the king or the president of this city?

What job shall the saints will do? What will you do if this city becomes yours? If you ask me, I cannot answer you now. But today's life will determine tomorrow's destiny.

It is a challenge to you and must seriously decide your stand today for the coming city (the New Jerusalem).

Who must enter this city or have chance to be in this city? If you believe it or not, it is going to come. God is eternal God and whatever He creates is an eternal thing.

But sin destroys the nature of everything that is eternal. Means there is nothing that can destroy any created being but sin. So, God will destroy sin and sinner for eternity.

New Jerusalem will not be entered with anything that is sin. Those murderers; sexually immoral, idolaters, and whoever loves and practices a lie will be outside of the city. Sin will not be part in this city.

There will be no anything that will be the test for saints. The city will contain only good; perfect and precious things. Christ Jesus will be the leader; the king and president in this city. The city holds the glory of the Lord and of the Lamb. It is dwells justice and righteousness.

Those who dwell in have the character; the image and the likeness of God. There will be no second devil; for the former things are over and shall not be remembered.

There will be no lack; poverty, disease or anything such like that. For things are make new and former ones are forever forgetting. This city has no end and it will be there for countless age.

It is the city of God and it cannot be destroy or collapse. For God is eternal God and everlasting father. The saints will be like angels in power and excel in strength.

There will be no death but life will be their food every day. Their food will be life; drinks will be life, clothes will be life, shelters will be life and work will be life. Everything will be life for them.

There is no light off; water shortage, sun heat or any other thing that cause trouble to wellbeing. Life will be fruitful always and joy will be our food every day.

It is an everlasting city and peace reigns all the time. Discouragement; fruitless, burdens, worries and fears will not be heard off. There shall be no motherless; fatherless, widow, orphans in this city.

God shall be our father and mother throughout eternity. We shall see Him face to face and our tears will forever wipe away. We shall rest from all burdens and our good works shall follow us.

Let us fight and enter into the narrow way that leads to life. Let consider this text and discus something about it.

Isaiah 66:6-13

6The sound of noise from the city! A voice from the temple! The voice of the LORD, Who fully repays His enemies!

God will punish those who cause problem for the saints and oppression them. He will fully repay their enemies. Our eyes shall see the suffering of our enemies and they shall be tormented and vanish eternally.

Consider verse 7 and 8 for state that the everlasting city will be in. Read;

7"Before she was in labor, she gave birth; before her pain came, she delivered a male child.

8Who has heard such a thing? Who has seen such things? Shall the earth be made to give birth in one day? Or shall a nation be born at once? For as soon as Zion was in labor, she gave birth to her children.

Means in Zion or New Jerusalem there shall be no pain in anything that we will be doing. Our life shall be free from pain and hardships. Things will be easy and comfort. Whatever we will do, will be in joy and happiness. The situation will be pleasant and peace. Read verse 9 and 10.

9Shall I bring to the time of birth, and not cause delivery?" says the LORD. "Shall I who cause delivery shut up the womb?" says your God.

10"Rejoice with Jerusalem, and be glad with her, all you who love her; Rejoice for joy with her, all you who mourn for her;

Our life will out of pressure and chaos; all things will be easy for us. I mean those who have chance to enter the New Jerusalem. We shall forget the past and it will not come to mind or heart.

Our heart shall fill with joy and we rejoice with angels of heaven. There will be no more hunger but satisfaction. We shall drink deeply with abundance of glory.

We shall be at peace like a river and as the one whom his mother comforts. God will comfort us in the city of Jerusalem. Read verse 11; 12 and 13 and take note of the situation of the saints in the New Jerusalem.

11That you may feed and be satisfied With the consolation of her bosom, That you may drink deeply and be delighted With the abundance of her glory."

12For thus says the LORD: "Behold, I will extend peace to her like a river, And the glory of the Gentiles like a flowing stream. Then you shall feed; on her sides shall you be carried, and be dandled on her knees.

13As one whom his mother comforts, So I will comfort you; And you shall be comforted in Jerusalem."

Let us continue the reading and consider other truth concerning the state of the saints.

Isaiah 65:16-23

Verse 16; we shall bless ourselves in the Lord and shall swear by the Lord of truth. Our trials; our sadness, worries and troubles will be forgotten. It shall be hidden from our eyes and will not remember again. Read;

16So that he who blesses himself in the earth shall bless himself in the God of truth; and he who swears in the earth shall swear by the God of truth; because the former troubles are forgotten, And because they are hidden from my eyes.

This world will be forgotten and shall no more remember. God will create the new one and the former will not come to mind or be remembered. Jerusalem will be a rejoicing city and her people will be a joy. God shall rejoice with us and there shall be no more weeping or crying. For behold, he has created all things new. The city will be a joyful of city and her people will be a joy.

Death will be no more; everyone will be as God. That is, those who will be in the city. Our labor shall not be in vain. Neither shall anyone be plant for another to eat.

Jerusalem will last for eternity and her people shall also last for eternity. This city has no end; it has the age of God and His glory. Read verse 17 – 23 and consider the end message.

17"For behold, I create new heavens and a new earth; and the former shall not be remembered or come to mind.

18But be glad and rejoice forever in what I create; for behold, I create Jerusalem as a rejoicing, and her people a joy.

19I will rejoice in Jerusalem, and joy in my people; the voice of weeping shall no longer be heard in her, nor the voice of crying.

20"No more shall an infant from there live but a few days, Nor an old man who has not fulfilled his days; For the child shall die one hundred years old, But the sinner being one hundred years old shall be accursed.

21They shall build houses and inhabit them; they shall plant vineyards and eat their fruit. 22They shall not build and another inhabit; they shall not plant and another eat; for as the days of a tree, so shall be the days of my people, And My elect shall long enjoy the work of their hands.

23They shall not labor in vain, nor bring forth children for trouble; for they shall be the descendants of the blessed of the LORD, and their offspring with them.

I know you have heard and read some of the texts by yourself. What is your decision about this matter? How have you considered? What is your goal now? Which city do you wish to dwell?

This world will pass away and it shall never be remembered or comes to mind. New Jerusalem will be replacing by this world. It is a joy and everlasting city.

Money will not be necessary; luxurious cars will not be needed; airplanes will not be considered. Gold will be floor tiles on our foot. What again do you wish than this city?

17. What can we compare?

As God cannot be compare with anything, so is His dwelling place or city. New Jerusalem is the city of God and it is His kingdom. It is a city of His name and glory.

It has no likened and there is nothing that can be associated with from today's world. No human being can explain or describe. It was shown to John as human can know a little about it.

It is because God has prepared something for His love one which has never been in the heart of man or imagine. Who have seen God before and who can describe Him.

As God does not have any equal so is His city prepare for those who love Him. The city has the glory of God and it is also a light to this city. What can you imagine that will be equal to it.

It has been decorated with gold and other precious materials. It has a river of life; it has a tree of life, it has a sea of glass and different kinds of foundations with names of the Apostles written on it.

In it dwells righteousness and justice. It has equal in length; breadth and height. Three gates on each corner with angels; it gates does not shut and the walls are glasses. The sun; moon and stars are absent but only the glory of God is the light in this city.

Temple is not necessary, for God will be with His people and they shall serve Him all the time. Night will be absent; there will be no more pain, there will be no more sickness, there will be no more death.

There will be no more light bills; there will be no more school fees, there will be no more transport fairs, airplanes will not be necessary.

What can you compare or imagine with? No more tax collectors; no more metropolitan's assemblies whose cheat people for their own benefits.

No more militaries, no more police, no more fire service men and no more immigration service. There will no party or politicians who will seek for power. There will be no more prophets; pastors, teachers, magicians, doctors and others.

Supreme Court and high court will be absent and there shall be no more court registrar or secretary. Hospitals will be absent and mortuary will not be present. Harbor and others will be absent. Transports will be no more seen. Communication tools will not be necessary.

Football games and other entertainment will be absent. There will be no more thieves; fornicators, witchcrafts, occult, gangsters and other pleasurable activities.

All these and others that we see in today's world will not be present. This city new Jerusalem holds it peace and comfort. There shall be no more disturbances or any conflict among brothers.

Envy will be lost; murderers will be no more, bribe will not be present and cheating will be forever lost. Today's renowned cities will not be heard off. There shall be no lies; gambling and autocratic acts.

All that we hear and act in today's world will be absent. It is a city of God and anything that is unclean shall not enter. It is a joyful city and peace reigns.

Christ will be our king; leader or president and He will be light; joy and happiness. He shall reign forever and ever. What is your comfort and joy? Are you ready to be in this city?

For Good Living; salvation and Knowledge Gain!
B. B. S. LIFE BOOKS.

Also by Bernard Benson Sarfo

The Fact Among Facts (1st)
The Fact Among Facts

Standalone
The Youth Murderer
Be Original Not a Copy
The Christians Science or Scholarship
Precious than Paradise
Habit makes future
A shelter from storm and rain
The Science of Life
The Strongest Lion Knockback
The Perfect and Inspiring City
Above Hope, Faith and Love
The Hero's Brave Decisions
The Weakest Among Plants
The Hero's Brave Decisions
Doing Above The Ability
The Wisdom Beyond Power And Greatness

Heavier Than the Heavens
The Academics Brains and Recreation Logics

About the Author

Bernard Benson Sarfo is an acquainted architectural designer and a motivational speaker.He is a gifted teacher who continues to motivate and encourage many.

Read more at https://www.amazon.com//author/ bbslifebooks.

www.ingramcontent.com/pod-product-compliance
Lightning Source LLC
Chambersburg PA
CBHW031455130726
47989CB00003B/1408